Wall's
ICE CREAM

Alan Earnshaw,
David Hayward
&
Chris Stevens

Nostalgia Road Publications

CONTENTS

The **Nostalgia Road** Series ™

is produced under licence by

Nostalgia Road Publications Ltd.

Units 5 - 8, Chancel Place, Shap Road Industrial Estate,

Kendal, Cumbria, LA9 6NZ

Tel: +44 (0)1539 738832 - Fax: +44 (0)1539 730075

designed and published by

Trans-Pennine Publishing Ltd.

PO Box 10, Appleby-in-Westmorland, Cumbria, CA16 6FA

Tel: +44 (0)17683 51053 - Fax: +44 (0)17683 53558

e-mail: admin@transpenninepublishing.co.uk

and printed by

Kent Valley Colour Printers Ltd.

Kendal, Cumbria. Tel: +44 (0)1539 741344

© Text: Trans-Pennine Publishing Ltd. 2005
© Photographs: Author's collection or as credited

Front Cover: *Carrying bodywork by S.C. Cummins of Crewe (now a brand-name of Whitby Morrison), this is a long wheelbase Bedford CA equipped as a 'hard' ice cream van and operated by Manfredi's Ices of Worksop.* **Bryan Whitby**

Rear Cover Top: *The full details of Wall's delivery fleet, as opposed to mobiles, is little known, and many details still have to emerge. Here we see DAY 481Y, a Leyland 'Roadtrain' tractor unit with a Datum cab in Wall's sunshine and white livery.* **Chris Stevens Collection**

Rear Cover Bottom: *How the Wall's livery looks today, as the 'heart-brand' logo van appears on a Whitby Morrison-bodied Transit.* **Whitby Morrison**

Title Page: *Wall's had several Bedford-Scammell tractor units, both the OSS and SAG/SAO types. The multi-compartment trailer was unique however. Built on a Scammell drop-frame trailer with double rear wheels, it is seen at the Farnborough Air Show by the Blue Streak Rocket.* **Vauxhall Motors**

This Page: *A Morris J Type van, fleet number 1036, which was delivered new to Wall's in early 1950, and fitted with a body by Hooper. This may have been the first of its kind to be delivered as it is seen at the Friary, Acton.* **Wall's**

WALL'S ICE CREAM - AN INTRODUCTION

The next time you slurp on a Solero or crunch a Cornetto, you might like to reflect on the origins behind the world-leading brand of ice cream that you are eating, as the well-known Wall's name goes back almost 220 years. Many people will know of a vague connection with Wall's sausages, pies and meat products, even if only for the annoying little dog in the TV adverts that growls Wall's whilst pinching its master's favourite banger. Today the two brands are physically divorced from one another, as each is now owned and marketed by separate, large multi-national companies Kerry Group (the meat products) and Uni-Lever (the ice-cream and frozen foods). Of course our story is concerned with the ice-cream business, and this book follows the three other ice-cream titles from Nostalgia Road.

Ice-cream is, or at least was, a dessert; and at one time was one of the most exclusive and expensive desserts in the world (as told in our companion book *Fifty Years of Ice Cream Vehicles*). Yet, Wall's the story really begins with breakfast, the most staple meal of the day in Britain during the 16th to 19th centuries: in fact it was THE meal of the day, as history shows.

Above: *This picture is a superb indication of what life was like in a busy Wall's garage in the mid-1960s, as heavy delivery units on eight-wheel AEC chassis are interspersed with Mr.Whippy Commer BF ice-cream vans.* Wall's

For instance, the author Dr. Samuel Johnson recalls, a 'simple breakfast' for seven people held at Margaret Dodds' house in 1776. He later wrote that "even though the meal was served on a large buffet table, there were nine servants in attendance, five to fill our plates when first we went to the buffet and four to ensure that our plates would never again be empty."

The supposedly simple breakfast consisted of oatmeal with sweet cream, smoked herrings, sardines with mustard sauce, grilled trout with white butter sauce, cold veal pies, grilled kidneys, sausages with mashed potatoes, beef tongue with hot horseradish sauce, with (in Dr. Johnson's words) "enough bacon to feed a hungry army". It is interesting to note the breakfast use of cold meats, sausages and pies, as the humble pie was also used for many other meals at the time. Its use was especially noted among early travellers, and workmen who took their meals to their place of employment.

WALL'S ICE CREAM PUDDING

Left: *This well-known image clearly shows how Wall's ice-cream was 'mobiled' between the two World Wars. The idea for the trikes supposedly came from company Director Lionel Rodd, but cycling expert A. G. Hatter of Shoreham writes; "Wall's had been using delivery trikes in their meat and pie business in London since 1878. By 1902 they had 'cool box' trikes, in which dri-ice was used to provide an ambient temperature, especially in the summer months. This therefore may well have been the genesis for the ice-cream trike, or if not the idea was certainly not new to Wall's. The Singer company had been the firm's main supplier!"* Both Wall's

The pies of by-gone days had thick pastry 'walls', which ensured that meat pies could survive a long journey. Meanwhile, men working underground in places like the Cornish tin mines had their 'pasties' covered in a thick layer of tallow to make them waterproof. Often the top lid of pastry was removed from the pie before serving, as some people preferred to add additional seasoning or hot gravy. Sausages were another convenient way to cook and carry food on a journey, as they could be eaten cold or even baked in pastry to make a sausage roll. Mind you, most people would not even like to think about the kind or quality of the meat that went into many of these pies and sausages. However, if you are wondering what this has to do with ice-cream, don't worry, it is completely relevant.

The demand for good quality pies, sausages and cooked meats became increasingly evident in London's better classes of society, and to fill this niche market Richard Wall opened his successful business in St James's Market, London in 1786. He would go on to found the Wall's dynasty and become father to Thomas Wall, after whom the company would eventually be named. Richard very rapidly earned a reputation as a fine pork butcher and in 1812 he received the prestigious 'Royal Appointment to George, Prince of Wales' as a 'Purveyor of Pork. In the years that followed, the shop continued to serve His Majesty when he later became King George III.

Business prospects must have seemed good, and Richard decided the time was right to start a family, so Thomas arrived in 1817, followed by a sister, Eleanor, in 1824. The business was now becoming famous throughout London (and further afield) so he moved to larger more prestigious premises at 113, Jermyn Street. However, he worked long hard hours, and Richard died early leaving his widow, Ann, and the 19-year-old Thomas to run the business. They continued trading as Ann Wall & Son, but Ann died very shortly after and Thomas was left to take charge of both the business and his 14-year-old sister.

The young man took his responsibilities seriously and the business continued to thrive and in time he was able to marry and (at the age of 29) have his first son, Thomas Wall II, in 1846. Like his father and grandfather before him, young Thomas entered the pork butchery business, but did so as an apprentice. When this was completed in 1870, Thomas Wall took him fully into the business, which then traded as Thomas Wall & Son. The second son, Frederick, joined the management of the company in 1878 and the brand name was amended slightly to Thomas Wall & Sons. The business continued its high level of service and standards, and as a consequence received further Royal Warrants (or Appointments) from Queen Victoria, King Edward VII, King George IV and King George V. Which, in turn, stimulated other prestigious customers.

However, certain areas of the business were being 'nibbled' away by competitors, especially those firms that were supplying other products as a 'complete' service to their customers. The competitors that gave them most worry were (and still are) household names, namely The Express Dairy, Joseph Lyons and Sainsburys. Lyons were famous for their Corner Houses, cakes, teas and coffees, but in 1913 they entered the cooked meat and pie business, offering a 'comprehensive service' to the catering and retail outlets that they supplied.

Above: *Although this is a very poor picture, it shows the Southampton Depot c1947, with one of the war-time Fordson BBE delivery vans.* Wall's

The Barham family, who owned the Express Dairy Company, were very good friends with the Sainsbury family, and there had been talks of a possible merger between the two companies since the days of Queen Victoria. These very nearly came to fruition just before World War I, in what was described as a 'merger to resist the Lyons combine'. As both of these potentially huge rivals threatened to strangle the market, by 'comprehensive service', it left T. W. Wall & Sons facing a potentially dire threat to their 'relatively' seasonal business.

There can be no doubt that the pork trade was seasonal, as many people simply refused to eat such products during the summer months for such was the notoriety of pork in the days before home refrigeration became common. Ronald Davies of East Finchley, whose father was a salesman for Wall's back in the period 1909-44, says "my father always claimed he was the man who got Wall's into selling ices; true, not ice-creams, but frozen drinks, as he was instrumental in starting the sale of fruit concentrates to the cafes, hotels and shops that he 'travelled' to in the West End".

Ronald, continued "Many of these were loyal Wall's customers, and had been for years, and they wished to remain so. So father kept reporting that diversification into selling 'other lines' was essential. Through one of his trade-contacts, Wall's got the opportunity to import fruit concentrates from America, and my father was given the job of co-ordinating the sales." Nothing is left in the company's records to substantiate this account, but at the Public Record Office in Kew, a ledger from the Ministry of War Supply dated 1916, states that Messrs T. W. Wall & Sons Ltd., were 'purveyors of tinned meats (pork and beef), tinned sausages (pork and beef), tinned milk powder and custard, and tinned fruit concentrates.'

So where, when and why did Wall's start a canning operation. The why is fairly easy to answer; there was a war on, and all Britain's major manufacturing concerns were directed towards producing consumables for both the troops and the civilian population! The other questions are not so easy to answer, and no reord seems to exist of the canning operation other than these two sketchy references, but they may well point the way to what happened after the war.

The war years, and its attendant loss of able-bodied male workers, saw the arrival of hundreds of female employees, several of whom were praised for their nimbleness and dexterity. Many of these 'girls' were 'let go' when the war ended, but a good number of them were to rejoin the business when ice-cream production started in the 1920s. There are conflicting stories about what happened next, and along with our fellow author on the ice-cream books, Steve Tillyer, we have reason to doubt the precise date at which the operation began.

The book *Licks, Sticks & Bricks* states: "In 1922 T. Wall & Sons began making ice-cream 'in the American way' in London". Other records state 1921 and 1923 as being the starting point, however, a significant even occurred in America during the summer of 1920, when Ernest A. Hamwi took out a US-patent (1,342,045) for an ice-cream-cone-making machine. Hamwi had already shown off his idea at the 1904 World's Fair, but the invention got 'lost sight of' in the years that followed.

His invention was important to the growing confectionery trade in the USA, and England as well, because prior to this most ice-cream vendors sold their products in serving glasses called 'penny licks' (because you'd lick the ice-cream from the glass, and it cost a penny to do so). This was naturally a major health problem, but many people would accidentally break the glasses, or not so accidentally walk off with them. The 'penny lick' was thus a costly business. Hamwi's stand at the 1920 Trade Fair therefore attracted many overseas visitors.

Interestingly this included two 'large firms from London, one of whom sells beverages and cakes, the other a firm of meat suppliers.' This tantalising note may suggest that both Wall's and Lyons had caught on to the idea. The rest of the story is already told in our book *Fifty Years Of Ice Cream Vehicles*, and therefore need not be repeated here, save to say that once the equipment for ice-cream and cone/wafer-making had been brought to Britain, Wall's began circulating their customers with details of the new service. The first major mailshot was dated June 1922, but it appears that some preliminary marketing had been going on for many months prior to that. This in turn suggests that the equipment had been installed in the early part of 1921, but 'the jury is still out' on that one.

As the pictures on page four show, the main marketing tool of Wall's Ice Cream was the 'Walsie Trike', which became common sights all over the more-populated parts of Britain. In the days when the street-trading or 'mobiling' of ice-cream was done either by hand-cart or horse and cart, the trikes were a novel, inexpensive way to saturate the market. The numbers grew rapidly, and Wall's replenished the salesmen on bikes by using a fleet of Model T and Model A Ford vans, pictures of which are seen later. By the summer of 1938 there was a fleet of around 8,600 trikes, whilst a further 15,000 shops stocked the company's products as well.

After a year of hostilities, ice-cream vans and trikes vanished off the streets almost overnight as the summer drew to a close in 1940. Not only was the seasonal trading about to slow down for the winter, but it would be some five years before it would re-awaken. Rationing of both petrol and sugar would play a dramatic part in the hibernation of this industry during World War II, but the vehicles previously employed in it were not left idle. By 1939, the Walls 'trikes' had grown into a massive fleet, and many were handed over for the 'national good'. Some became delivery bikes with the Post Office, and at least 100 were handed over to the Women's Voluntary Service for use as emergency feeding stations. These were used to carry tea urns, sandwiches and sticky buns to railway stations in order to 'feed' troops being moved by rail, or to take sustenance to places where enemy bombing had destroyed local facilities.

Other trikes were allocated to the navy shore base HMS *Harrier* in Pembrokeshire, where they were used as ground-to-air control training units, at a time when every serviceable aircraft was needed for operational work. A Wren would pretend to be a pilot and the trainee controllers would direct the various 'planes into either landing, take-off or attack positions. Naturally 'mid-air' collisions were frequent!

Awakening From World War II

The brave front of trying to keep on 'mobiling' during the summer of 1940, soon saw the two main Wall's factories being given over to the production of margarine, following the banning of milk and dairy products for use in ice-cream in the autumn of that year. The main bulk delivery fleet remained intact however, and it was used for the delivery of margarine, tinned fruit concentrates and meat products during the war. Interestingly, the production of blocks of margarine were said to be 'good preparation for the post-war production of ice-cream of the Eskimo Pie type.' However, even when the war ended, the supplies of many basic raw materials, especially those that were imported, were restricted due to two factors; these being the balance of payments crisis and the shortage of merchant vessels, due to the numbers of ships that had been sunk during the war.

Above: *The use of trikes had seen several limitations in the pre-war days, notably the distance over which they could operate. So, whilst the trike fleet was re-built from 1946 onwards, more thought was given to 'mobiling' with motor vehicles. The Austin FX chassis, such as we see on this prototype bodied by Hooper, provided the ideal type to cope with the rugged stop-start work of an ice-cream van.* Wall's

Problems with supplies of milk, sugar and cream were to continue until 1953, so Wall's used its margarine technology to produce ice-cream using blends of vegetable oil and sugar. Sperm whale oil was also used for a while, but cod-liver oil was instantly discounted on account of its 'distinctive' taste. Even when rationing ended in 1953, the company continued to largely use vegetable oils, because (according to *Licks, Sticks and Bricks*) "the British public had grown used to the taste."

Top Left: *This view shows what is a rather rare beast in ice-cream van form at least, as it is an Austin A70 Hampshire, which was only built between 1948 and 1950.* C. K. Bowers

Middle Left: *As mentioned earlier, the Austin FX chassis (normally used for London taxi cabs) had a petrol engine that was ideal for stop-start work, once again the body on the FX3 seen here is by Hooper.* C. K. Bowers

Bottom Left: *In addition to the main purchases from Austin, Wall's showed keen interest in the new Morris J-Type, which had a chassis price of £220, when launched in 1947-8. One is seen here with a Hooper body.* C. K. Bowers

The truth may well be found in another explanation, for the price of vegetable oil was far less than comparable supplies of dairy fats. At the height of rationing in 1950-2, Wall's used a combined total of over 18,000-tons of vegetable and fish oil, aggregating to around 6,000-tons per annum. According to a Wall's press release in April 1959, the company's ice-cream products used 98% vegetable oil. However, new labelling laws were soon to change all of that, as they stipulated any product containing the word 'Dairy Ice-cream' on the packaging had to be made with dairy fats. By the end of 1960, Wall's annual usage of vegetable oil had dropped to 3,800 tons, despite an increase in production. In its place came 2,000-tons of butter, with the vegetable oil content dropping to between 50% and 72% depending on the type of product.

To sell their products, Wall's needed to develop a new fleet of 'mobiles', and it was obvious to them that the trike had had its day. Motorising was the answer, but although the sales area covered was greatly enhanced, and takings up as a result, the cost of a motor vehicle was considerably higher than a trike.

The first experiments began for the summer season of 1947, using a modified version of a pre-war Austin 12hp 1500cc chassis. Yet, this proved to be under-powered, and something more rugged was needed, so they started using Austin's 2199cc-engined A70 Hampshire. This probably was supplied as a pick-up, but we do know that in addition to being a saloon (costing £608), it was also available as an estate and later as a chassis-scuttle. In total, just 35,261 Hampshire models were built. The body was built by the famous London coachbuilders, Hooper & Son, so this combination would not have been a cheap 'mobile' and may have cost around about a four-figure sum at the time. Nevertheless, it is known that Austin A70 Hereford and Austin A40 (both Somerset and Dorset) models were later used.

Costing slightly less, but more economical in operation, was the Austin FX3 taxi chassis and around 90 of these were used in the Wall's fleet. Thirty of them were based in Manchester alone, and others are known to have been used in London, Birmingham, Glasgow and Bristol. Even so, cost was still an issue, tyre wear was heavy, and so too was fuel consumption. What Wall's needed was a light commercial van that could be easily converted into a 'mobile'. A batch of Trojan vans were tested, but these were not well-liked and no more were bought.

Then Morris Commercial introduced the J-Type 10-cwt model at the 1948 Earls Court Commercial Motor Show, although the van seen at the show differed in many ways from the production vehicles that were to follow in the autumn of 1949. A large number of these would enter the Wall's fleet between 1950 and 1956. Body conversions were done by Hooper, Wadham Stringer, Morrison, and Scotts.

Austin were however still in the frame and slightly ahead of Morris, for in 1948 they launched their K8 25-cwt van. Thanks to its unusual body, with double doors on the nearside, offside, and rear, it became known as the 'Three-Way van'. Wall's immediately took to this versatile beast, and Hoopers compartmentalised the body for them. The load-space was divided in half, with the rear portion being a 'cold store' accessed by the rear doors. The near-side door provided an entry/exit for the salesman, and the off-side door was replaced with a 'barn door' arrangement. When this was opened out, it gave a sales stand, price boards and a canopy for the vendor; as is seen in the pictures right. However, the K8 only remained in production until 1954, for following the merger of Austin and Morris, it was replaced by the LD model.

Top and Middle Right: *The ubiquitous Austin K8 'mobile', seen with the doors closed for travelling, or open for 'mobiling'. In addition to the use of these in the street sales fleet, Wall's also used the Three-Way van for delivering meat products as well. A larger version of the K8, the CXB/CXD bus chassis, for a much larger type of mobile sales unit was used, as will be shown later. C. K. Bowers*

Bottom Right: *Prior to researching this part of the book, we believed that Wall's had stuck entirely to Austin or Morris chassis for its 'mobiling' fleet; but at the eleventh hour, we found this image of a Commer Superpoise. The 25- to 30-cwt chassis provided a good base on which to build a mobile shop, and it is apparent that other Rootes models were used in the years ahead, but not in large numbers. C. K. Bowers*

As we will discuss presently, the Morris LD of 1953 swept into the Wall's fleet, almost to the extent that it, along with the Morris J, became the standard unit. This of course made sense, as standardisation was a great assistance to both the fitters and the cost of spares that needed to be held in the depots. Of course, the sales around this time were still based on frozen drinks on a stick, or ice-creams made with vegetable oils. To get around the problems with rationing and vehicle allocation, Wall's attempted to turn their confectionery into a food item, with the new sales drive, 'More Than A Treat - A Food'. Yet, by the end of the 1950s, a new trend would affect production methods, as a demand began to emerge for powdered ice-cream 'mix'.

Alfred Baker, a worker at the Craigmillar Factory near Edinburgh, recalls the period: "All of a sudden, we had real competition, and these new 'soft' ices were all the rage. About ten years after we had opened we noticed that our production figures dropped, and as a trade union representative, I was asked to see the bosses. All the staff were worried by what was happening, and with the company building a new factory at Gloucester, we thought we would be 'for the chop' and that was the way it eventually worked out, not only for Craigmillar, but for Manchester as well!" The issue of 'soft-ice' would change Wall's perspectives for good in the early 1960s, but in the late 1940s and early 1950s, they were selling all they could produce.

Left and Top Right: *The quest for better, cheaper ways of 'mobiling' saw the Wall's company investing in electric vehicle technology. These two images show the front and rear aspects of one of the larger vans supplied by Morrison Electricar of Southampton in or around 1959. It has fleet number 2778, and is even provided with a litter bin in the front near-side door. Around the same time, a similar vehicle was supplied for evaluation by Smith's Electric Vehicles of Gateshead.* Both Whitby Morrison

Middle Right: *The desire to use technology current in the milk-delivery industry saw Wall's experiment with Brush Battery Electric Vehicles. In 1947 this Loughborough company, famous as a maker of trams, began to heavily promote the Brush Pony, a lightweight 'electric float' in the 5- to 8-cwt capacity. Note how this Wall's ice-cream float (E1) carries a semi-open body.* Whitby Morrison

Bottom Right: *The next step in design came with fleet number E2, which now has a cab, although the 'serving body' still has open doorways on both sides.* Whitby Morrison

The sales of Wall's ice-cream changed after the war, and in 1947 the company sold 3,300 of its trikes and invested the money in 762 Sterne freezer cabinets to be installed in retail shops. This gave them 'year-round' sales, whereas the trikes had been mainly seasonal. By this time 90% of production was being sold via retail outlets, and only 10% by 'mobiles', and Wall's may well have gone out of the 'mobiling' business altogether. The target audience was the entertainment market, as people 'let their hair down' after six-years of wartime conditions. "Only the Yanks had ice-cream during the last years of the war" recalls P.B. Walters who was a salesman based at Wall's Barnstaple Depot, "and the British lads coming back from the forces, demanded it be on sale wherever they went to enjoy themselves. Silly as it sounds, it was a way to impress the girls. We got orders to target dance halls, theatres, restaurants and above all, to people at home."

By 1953, when rationing ended, the company had in excess of 35,000 outlets selling ice-cream products. These were in addition to the final company-owned trikes, and a slowly growing number of motorised 'mobiles'. The year 1948 was another significant time for Mr. Walters, for as he recalls: "Uni-Lever began an advertising campaign test in Barnstaple, where we sold on the basis that 'ice-cream was more than a treat - it was a food' to encourage home consumption."

Above and Left: *The depots in the West Country were chosen to test a new type of 'mobiling' concept, as there were a number of static kiosks located along the coastal resorts in Devon and Cornwall. Added to this, a few trikes were still working in the more popular resorts, and the means of provisioning these was causing problems. As a result Wall's produced a number of 'combined delivery-mobiling' units. As the name implies, these were vans that could both carry bulk stocks in a freezer compartment, and at the same time 'mobile' from a small sales area at the back. Two types were tried, both with Morrison bodywork. The first was the standard Austin-Morris LD, a rugged but dour offering from the British Motor Corporation. Here we see two views of fleet 2701 (666 WHX), which dates from the ninth batch of these vehicles in 1959.*
Both Whitby Morrison

Right: *The LD chassis-cowl, introduced to the Wall's fleet in 1953 was perfect as a conventional 'mobile', but in reality even the 30-cwt version struggled in the role of a dual-purpose vehicle. More practical was the Rootes Group's Karrier Gamecock, which was rated at 30-cwt to two-ton. As can be seen from the pictures here, this chassis allowed for a much larger 'storage area' in both terms of length and height. Registered 621 TMD, number 1542 was first registered in October 1958.* Both Whitby Morrison

Although the Barnstaple campaign was repeated nationally, and Wall's gained another 6,000+ retail outlets, the idea of 'mobiling' direct to the public had not entirely been forgotten. Once again, Barnstaple Depot was chosen for an experiment during the 1959 summer-season, as it had a large number of outlets along the north Devon and Somerset coastlines.

As Mr Walters reveals: "Wall's were achieving all their targets, but they wanted not only the toffee but the ha'penny as well. So in addition to selling to sea-front retailers, we also entered direct competition with them. To do this, Wall's purchased a number of small mobile trailer kiosks, from a firm called Picador of Sholing. These were positioned all around the West Country on the popular tourist beaches, and we supplied them with a Model 52 Ford van. The problem was that this pre-war van was 'clapped out', and it was working from about 5am to 3pm, delivering loads of ice-cream to replenish the kiosks in the height of the summer season. As a result we asked for (and received) something better. The idea came from our depot manager at the time, who had the idea for a delivery van that could carry enough stock to stock-up all the kiosks and shops on a selected route on a daily basis. The vans we had were a Karrier and a Morris, and these either ran west or north to north-east along the coast. The Morris worked west to Bude, where it terminated, whilst the Karrier had the tortuous hilly road from Ilfracombe to Blue Anchor Bay. When the vans had supplied all their kiosks and shops en-route, they then became static 'mobiles', dispensing ices from a little sales cabin at the back. Another Karrier was added to the fleet the following season"

It is understood that other depots with resort areas were supplied with similar vans after the Barnstaple trials, but around this time Wall's had about 175 depots, up on the 160 that it had used in the pre-war period. Barnstaple got two more of these combined vans in the late-1950s, but by that time all five were from the Routes Group stable. The LDs were re-allocated to East Anglia, where there were fewer hills to cope with than the Devon banks.

THE 1950S & '60S

During the late-1950s, television advertising became an important medium for the company, and by clever marketing the sales continued to go through the roof. The 'Wallsie' brand was an important gimmick, as the cartoon featured on both TV and cinema commercials. By 1955 the country was already eating one-million gallons of ice-cream a year and the factories at Acton, Gloucester, Craigmillar and Godley (Manchester) were at full production by the end of the decade. A joint biscuit bakery was opened with Lyons at Gloucester, but already tastes were changing and a significant threat loomed on the horizon.

Above: *The Wall's product, throughout the 1950s had been the traditional 'hard' ice-cream products, and the success of the brand saw it being exported to many overseas countries, such as this left-hand-drive Morris LD for Saudi Arabia.* Wall's

This new threat, combined with the increased facilities at Gloucester, would lead to the closure of the Craigmillar and Godley plants in the early 1960s. It was of course, 'soft' ice-cream, introduced to the UK around the same time by two rivals. The story is well told in the books by our colleague, Steve Tillyer in *The Mr.Whippy Story* and *The Mister Softee Story*; both of which are available in the Nostalgia Road series.

Right: *Although this series of images was used in our book* Fifty Years of Ice Cream Vehicles, *we have no hesitation in showing them again here, as they demonstrate the layout of the early Morrison-bodied BMC LDs that were used to sell Wall's 'Super Whip' ice-cream.*
Both Whitby Morrison

The basic concept behind 'soft' ice-cream was the fact it was made on the vehicle, using electrically-driven machinery. The leading manufacturer of this equipment was the Italian company Carpigiani, and this had long been used in static locations like ice-cream parlours and restaurants. Two American brothers, the Conway's, are credited with the idea of taking such equipment out of a static location and fitting it in to a 'mobile'. Powered by an on-board generator, using a separate engine, these 'mobile Mister Softee factories' soon became a great hit in the USA. Both Mr.Whippy and Mister Softee lay claim to bringing the idea to Britain in 1959, but for all intents and purposes they were more or less simultaneous with one another.

The real point of the story, is the fact that Wall's were caught with their pants down. Mister Softee, was in fact an idea introduced by Gateshead vehicle manufacturers, Smith's, who had seen the idea in the States and brought it to Britain in the hope of selling more vehicle bodies. In turn, Smith's, struck up a deal with the Rootes Group to use the Commer 30-cwt to two-ton chassis, as this was considered the minimum size to carry the additional weight of the generators (fuelled by Tractor Vapourising Oil or TVO) that would be needed. One of the Smith family told us that, they "first approached Wall's with the idea in 1958, but were laughed out of the office, so we went to see Lyons, who took us much more seriously - in the end, we were the ones with the smile on our face," he added.

The other contender was Dominic Facchino, who imported the idea and marketed it in Britain as the Mr. Whippy franchise. This business would later be taken on by multi-millionaire Charles Forte, although a half-share in the business was eventually sold to Wall's as from 1st January 1964. Yet for five years the 'soft' ice-cream onslaught left Wall's rocking and reeling. Arguably it can be said that the company's overall sales did not decline markedly, but their share of the market did not rise; the market was in fact growing and Wall's were not keeping up. To compete, it launched its own 'Soft Whip' brand, but management decided to stick to the BMC LD chassis. Donald Hayle, an engineer at Wall's recalls: "This was a stupid idea, the back end of the LD chassis just could not carry the weight of the generator, and they kept breaking off as a result."

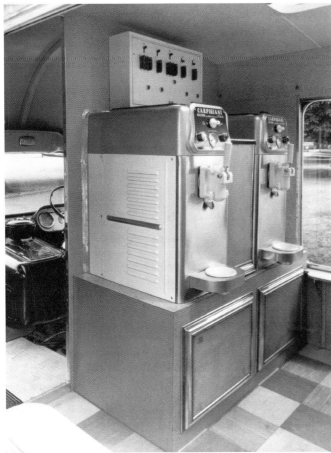

Left: *The idea of large rear-end generators was problematic for Wall's, as the back of LD chassis was quite inadequate for the weight it was being asked to carry. Yet a decision was made to stick with the LD, as the firm intended to convert over 60% of its existing 'hard' vans to 'Soft Whip mobiles'. It was therefore decided to mount the Carpigiani machines amidships between the two axles, and use a smaller generator mounted below the floor. The two machines could not however be used at the same time, as the generator did not simply have enough load on it, and it easily overheated in the confined location in which it was situated.* Both Whitby Morrison

Donald Hayle continues: "During the winter of 1960-1, I was given the instruction to try and install the generator in-between the wheels, but the large 12.5kva models were a physical impossibility. There was talk of 'stretching the chassis' to extend the wheelbase, but this would have created new 'weak-spots' and wasn't in my opinion worth pursuing. Just as we were about to admit defeat, Onan brought out a new 5kva generator, which was about half the size of the one we had been playing with. We slung one of these under the floor between the wheels, and mounted two 'soft ice' machines above it. It worked to a fashion, but there was really only enough power output for one machine at a time, and whilst it was useful to have a second in reserve, its extra weight was a serious drawback on a 30-cwt chassis. The picture (top left) shows the prototype we rigged up, and I believe this ran on 'test' for several months, but generally only one machine was installed in the vans that followed.

The other big problems were ones of noise, vibration and smell. The sales cabin was a bad environment after the Onan was installed beneath the floor, and you could almost taste the TVO fumes in the ice-cream. The operator who worked with us on the test, Steve Thomas, used to come back each day looking as white as a sheet and complaining of a blinding headache. So this was obviously not the way forward. About this time, we had in a batch of MkI Bedford CA 'mobiles' that had come from a small business that Wall's had acquired in the Nottinghamshire area. Our job was to strip these out of their ice-cream fittings and sell them on as second-hand mobile shops (we did not want to encourage private competitors by selling used ice-cream vans). One of these vans was stripped down to the chassis and we strengthened the back end, so that it would accommodate the Onan 5kva generator. Morrisons built a new body using, where possible, lightweight materials including a fibreglass roof. This became fleet number 6416, and the vanguard of a very large Bedford CA fleet."

Around this time, the company's Chief Mechanical Engineer began to take an interest in the project, and Mr. Hayes was asked to take him out on a 'mobiling' run for three days. The van was tested at Henley during the Regatta week, but it moved from point to point, following the crowds and thus was not static. The end result was a resounding 'thumbs-up', which in turn led to orders being placed with Vauxhall Motors, the manufacturer of the Bedford CA van.

Leo Kane, then in the sales team at Bedford remembers the order: "It was early in 1961 when the deal went through, and it had the potential of being around 250 CAs a year. Wall's had tested a MkI CA of their own, which they thought was ideal for the job they wanted. Yet, this model was only rated at 10- to 12-cwt, and had needed strengthening at the back end to carry additional equipment. By that time we had launched the MkII version, which was considerably more potent, it had a bigger engine, a stronger 12- to 15-cwt chassis and a better floor pan in the cab. It also had a one-piece windscreen, removing a potential 'blind-spot' that had been evident on the MkI. We were asked to supply CALZ (chassis cowl) models at the rate of 50 per month, between December and April. They were to be delivered direct to three body-builders, the main one was in Southampton, and they took 30 at a time, one was in Scotland, who were to take 10 a month, and the other was in the Midlands and they also received 10 a month."

The secret in getting the most out of a 15-cwt chassis was to use a lightweight body, and the only way to achieve this was by discarding the traditional ash frame and aluminum panel method and use a total glass-fibre. But at this stage, none of the conventional builders were interested in looking at the concept, especially Wadham Stringer and Hooper, who had done so much for Wall's in the past.

Right: *Here we have two views of the modified MkI Bedford CA, which was modified in the company's workshops and fitted with an Onan 5kva generator set. This was mounted on a strengthened 'chassis tail', as the normal 10- to 12-cwt frame was considered to be too weak to hold it. Four struts of four-inch box section and some 'L-angle' section were used to hold the generator. In turn this was accessed by a large rear door seen in the bottom picture. The generator sat under the counter at the back of the 'mobile', and it was 'vented' by the small mesh grille seen below the waistband. This later proved inadequate, and more ventilation was given to the production models. An all-glassfibre roof reduced the weight of the body, but the overall load was still a heavy one. Whitby Morrison*

Left: *The Morris (later BMC) LD van was a major part of the Wall's fleet during the 1950s and early-1960s, and these views show it in various forms within the fleet. The top one shows it in use as a Soft Whip van, displaying the 'Walsie' logo and the traditional Wall's slogan, 'Stop Me and Buy One'. It is taking part in the Lorry Driver of the Year Competition in 1963.*
Chris Stevens (top and centre), Whitby Morrison (bottom)

Launched in July 1953, the Morris LD replaced the pre-war Morris PV series and was initially only available as a petrol-engined, one-ton (20cwt) model. However, its 235 cubic foot body could be readily converted to an ice-cream 'mobile' and did not need to be specially bodied. Wall's acquired both complete vans and chassis cowls, and the difference between the two can be seen in photographs of the period. In 1953 BMC launched the Austin-Morris LD2, a 30-cwt, cubic foot version, which was both longer and taller. In 1955, the van received a new front-end styling, and a diesel-engine option could be fitted; large numbers of LDs were purchased in both forms.

The LD then remained the front-line 'mobiling' unit into the 1960s, but the Commer BF in the Whippy and Softee fleets caused Wall's to think again. The LD was not suited for 'soft' ice-cream work, and when the Mr.Whippy brand was acquired in 1964, all the remaining LDs were turned over to 'hard' ice-cream sales, and the new Bedford CAs entered the fray as 'soft' vans. To provide a nimbler, cheaper kind of 'hard', van, both Wall's and Lyons Maid began looking at light commercial vehicles that were being derived from cheap family saloon cars, and in these the BMC Morris Minor 1000, the BMC Mini, the Vauxhall Viva/Bedford HA, and the Ford Anglia 107E/Thames 307E were the main contenders. For around £500, plus £250 for conversion, such vehicles could be put out on the streets to compete with the new 'soft' ice-cream vans.

The alternative was a low-cost vehicle, selling traditional 'hard' products at a price less than those on the Whippy/Softee Commer BFs, and this concept very nearly worked. Wall's saw Ford's 307E five-cwt Thames van (based on the Anglia) as the ideal vehicle, but it had a major drawback, as to operate it the vendor had to stand outside the vehicle, because there was insufficient room inside the vehicle; despite the fact that three different types of 'bandstand' cabin were tried on the cut-down van body. A number of left-hand-drive 308E models were also used, so the driver could serve from his seat, but even these were prone to difficulties. Some seven-cwt vans of the 309E/310E model designations were also purchased, again including both rhd and lhd variations.

Above: *The Ford Thames 307E van, was a novel concept in low-cost 'mobiling'. Three types of body style were employed, and all of them retained the two-door cab layout. However, after these vehicles had been in service for a while it was discovered that they contravened health regulations, as they did not have a sink inside for the operator to wash his or her hands. In the absence of room, the nearside door was removed and 'skinned' over, and a sink inserted in a unit on the inside of the door. The work was done in three Wall's depots, and in one of these former properties, a cache of 200 left-hand doors were found in a loft in 1997. They were a pleasant surprise for owners of preserved Ford vehicles.* Whitby Morrison

Right: *An uncommon variation of the Wall's light 'mobile' van is seen on this 1966 Morris Minor LCV.* Eddie Farrell

WALL'S WHIPPY

As mentioned earlier, the full story behind Mr. Whippy is told in Volume Seven of this series, but through this brand Wall's acquired a new breed of 'mobiler', the independent franchisee. One of them, Daisy Reynolds, picks up the story.

"In 1959 Vic Haddert, who was the representative for Dominic Facchino at that time, persuaded Ken (Reynolds) that his future was to purchase a Mr. Whippy van, a revolutionary way of producing ice-cream on the round. Ken put in his order, but this was at the same time as he was purchasing his first house, which was costing £2,250.00 whilst the van was £3,120.00. Looking back we can't believe we would take such a gamble. The great day dawned – the van arrived. Neighbours and passers-by marvelled at seeing ice-cream produced before their eyes. After some preliminary instruction on how to pull a cornet and sterilise the machine, Ken was ready to do his round with his wonderful new van. What bliss – no more inserts, the ice-cream was kept in freezers, so it didn't have to be unloaded every night, and it kept in excellent condition.

Above: *The above picture shows Ken Reynolds with his dad Bill, outside their shop on William Street, Grays, Essex, in the 1950s. The Fordson E83W and Bedford CA vans had no freezers and operated with 'inserts', which meant several trips had to be made back to the shop to change them. Invariably the ice-cream was in a real runny state by the time the exchange was made. Also the return enabled them to replenish the stock of 1d lollies, which Bill Reynolds would be making in the general grocery shop.* Daisy Reynolds

When we think of the condition of some of the ice-cream we used to sell before freezers it makes you cringe, but nobody seemed to suffer any ill-effects. If a customer had a member of the family on night work, they put a card in their window with a large N on it, so we would know not to sound the chimes in the immediate vicinity. Instead we would give that customer either a flash of the headlights directly into their window or a very light toot on the horn, to let them know we were outside. Even so, we never stopped directly outside that particular house, even if it was a regular call.

On the round people would watch in amazement as Ken pulled off six to eight cones in one hand. Customers were so disciplined they would form queues at his stops well in advance of his arrival. Life had changed drastically. Work began at 8.30am each morning, cleaning the vans and sorting out any orders. The round started at 10.00 and went on till 10.15pm, then the machine had to be washed out and sterilised before returning home, so the day didn't end till around 11.00pm and that was seven days a week.There was the time when there was no electricity at the local hospital and we were called upon to take our Mr.Whippy vans (we had three of them by then) over there to generate electricity for the operating theatre, which we felt rather proud and pleased to do."

Daisy also recalls her involvement in those early days: "We were courting at this time and my project was to sit on the freezer while Ken was driving and hang on to the roof for fear it would lift off and disappear. How well we remember covering the Orsett Show, a major event in the area, with Blackjacks and dri-ice operating from kiosk's which took a week to get ready, transport and assemble."

Mobilers like Ken and Daisy became very important to Wall's, especially after they bought out the entire shares of the Whippy brand from Forte in 1966. It was still a massive loss-making operation for Wall's, but they gradually began to turn it around, whilst continuing to make better profits from the 'hard' vans and retail shop outlets. They had protected their market share, but only at a significant cost.

Top Right: *For 1966, the all-fibreglass bodies (with the lightweight Onan generators at the back) were THE way for Wall's to take on their main rival, Lyons Maid, who with their Mister Softee brand were still using the heavy Commer BF chassis for their main fleet. Branded as both Wall's and Mr.Whippy mobiles, these CAs are seen outside the Ice Cream Alliance Show at Buxton.* Ice Cream Alliance

Centre and Bottom Right: *Although the advent of Bryan Whitby's patent for a direct drive ice-cream system is told in* Fifty Years of Ice Cream Vehicles, *we need to emphasize just how important this was for the industry. Using a power-take-off (PTO) unit on the vehicle's engine allowed operators to dispense with the additional (and weighty) generator. From 1965-onwards, this was the way to go, and the Bedford CA, and the later CF models shown here, were far more cost-effective than the lumbering Commers with their heavy TVO-fuelled generators .* Whitby Morrison

MOBILING ON

By the mid-1970s the sales of ice-cream products in supermarkets and home freezer-ownership had radically altered the 'mobiling' market, and Wall's decided to stop operating the Mr.Whippy vans as company-owned vehicles. A lot of these were scrapped at Sharpness Dock in order to prevent them being used by 'competitors', whilst the newer vans were then offered to people who wanted to take on a Mr.Whippy franchise. After acquiring the brand outright in 1966, the number of vans had climbed steadily to about 1,600, and by the end of the 1970s, there were still around 1,000 independent Mr.Whippy vans who were 'supplied their soft-ice mix by Wall's.'

The 1970s had a few warm summers, and with growing affluence, impulse sales were up on previous years. It was however in the area of 'character' products that the greatest success was seen, especially as cartoon characters like Tom & Jerry and Spiderman influenced a new era of salesmanship. The changes that followed would become legendary, with all kinds of new brands appearing to satisfy the 'discerning palate'; 'soft' ice-cream, although still in great demand, was yesterday's child. It would take a book on its own to tell the story of what has happened at Wall's in the past two decades, and if there is sufficient public demand, we might just well do one in the future. Suffice it to say, names like the Cornetto and Solero brands, which we mentioned at the outset of the book, are now firmly embedded in the history of Wall's Ice Cream.

Top and Middle Left: *The Bedford CF II was just as popular with ice-cream men as the MkI CF and the CA had been before it. In fact, a number of these venerable machines from the 1980s are still to be found hard at work. Their fibreglass bodies are of course rust-free, whilst companies like Adrian Bailey from Leeds still manage to find and supply the mechanical parts to keep them on the road; especially following the demise of Bedford Trucks in the late-1980s.* Authors Collection

Bottom Left: *Today, the principle supplier of 'mobile' vehicles in this country is the firm of Whitby-Morrison from Crewe. Operated by Stuart Whitby (son of Bryan), this progressive company offers a variety of body styles. Ford Transits are of course a popular choice, with the Mercedes Sprinter following behind. Seen here wearing the Carte D'Or branding, this kind of Whitby van can also be seen in other Wall's liveries.* Whitby Morrison

SHOWING OFF

In the post-war era, Wall's may well have gone out of 'mobiling' altogether, had it not been for the phenomenal sales it generated at special events and shows. To capture this market, it built a number of special 'sales and enquiry' units, two of which are shown here. The upper picture (courtesy Whitby Morrison) is a 'special sales' body on a Scammell drop-frame Mechanical Horse trailer. The other (courtesy C.K. Bowers) is an Austin CXB/CXD light bus chassis with Hooper bodywork. Note how the back has been made to open out and allow a set of drop-down steps to be used. The 'barn-door' arrangement is of course familiar from the Austin K8 model pictured on page nine. Interestingly, this vehicle was jointly-owned/used by the ice-cream and sausage divisions of T. W. Wall & Sons.

The benefits of these sales units persuaded Wall's not to go entirely down the route of selling only through retail units, and they soon ended up with an administration section dedicated to only deal with show and event organisers. All the big outdoor countryside and sporting events were included, and this of course remains a key market area for the company today.

Smaller, local events were left to the depots to deal with, but given the fact that there were between 160 and 175 depots during the late-1940s/early-1950s, it comes as no surprise to find that around 400 small kiosk trailers were in the fleet. Whilst some depots did not have any trailers, most had at least one, but the busy seaside depots had several. These would be taken out at the start of the summer season and replenished daily. Few were towed back to a depot at night, as Roland Gill states: "Why did we need to take them back at night? Vandalism was unheard of in those days. Of course, we still had the birch for those who were willing to flaunt both laws and common decency."

Different kinds of mobile sales stands evolved in the 1960s, especially when the 'hard' ice-cream products were given a 'soft' edge. Steve Smith remembers, "I had a little Cornetto trailer that I could tow behind my car, an Austin Maxi. The Cornetto had come out in 1964-5, but it wasn't a success. However, by the early-1970s it had been re-introduced, and I could sell-out inside an hour of arriving at my pitch. My wife, then expecting our first baby, would slip back to the freezer to get more Cornettos and often made six or seven such trips in a day. Despite what the adverts said, there was no such thing as just ONE Cornetto."

Duncan Thomas sold Italian-style ice-cream from another mobile stand. "It was another success. I thought that the mixed blocks like Harlequin and Strawberry Fayre of the 1960s were brilliant, but Italiano ice-cream made me a lot of money at the time, although that was in the days before everybody else started selling 'soft-scoop' ices in a variety of exciting flavours.

Top Left: *A typical Picador trailer kiosk, made in Sholing, near Southampton.* Whitby Morrison

Middle Left: *The fashion for trailers had changed by the 1970s, as seen by this neat little unit dispensing Cornettos at 40-pence a time.* Stuart Birkby

Bottom Left: *Vaguely reminiscent of the Ford Thames 307E kiosk on wheels, this Wall's Italiano' stand looks to be doing a roaring trade under its red, white and green flags.* Stuart Birkby

Above: *Colour images of Wall's vehicles in the 1950s and '60s have proved rather elusive, especially images showing the powder blue and 'ice-cream' livery. The picture of the Bedford CA on the cover was painstakingly re-built and enhanced by computer technology from a cracked and faded original picture found behind a radiator. Another find was a series of pictures showing a small mobile high-top conversion on a 1971 FIAT 850 van, with Wall's only shield.* B. Smith

Right: *We make no excuse from again using the image seen in our book,* The Mr. Whippy Story *by Steve Tillyer, as it clearly shows the distinctive pink and white livery of the firm founded by Dominic Facchino in 1959. These Commer BF vans with Morrison bodies became part of the Wall's fleet, after they acquired an interest in the brand in 1964.* Peter Hopkins

Above: *The 'icicle pattern' continued beyond the 'powder blue and ice-cream' livery into what was known as the 'sunshine' livery. Here the cream paint was replaced by an ivory colour, whilst a 'sunshine' colour was used on the lower panels. These two pictures clearly demonstrate the variation between the 'shades' of 'sunshine' over the years. The upper van is a Morrison-bodied Bedford CF with a diesel engine. It also has a Mr.Whippy headboard, as the two brand identities were merged closer together and as the pink and white livery of the 'soft' vans was progressively abandoned. Whitby Morrison*

Left: *By contrast, here we have a Cummins Mk17 body, which was supplied by the Crewe builders to a franchisee in Chester. If this body is compared to the Cummins CA on the front cover, its origins can be clearly traced. Whitby Morrison*

Above: *Following the demise of S.C. Cummins, the Whitby family took on the brand name, as well as acquiring that of Morrison. Here we see a Ford Transit built by Whitby Morrison for Wall's in the late-1990s. An interesting fact about Morrison emerged during the clear-out of an office at the ill-fated (former Austin) plant at Longbridge in 2005, as a letter showed that Austin had taken a 50% interest in Morrison Electricar in 1948. This letter indicated that the business was worth acquiring, as "it had a new range of electric floats, being developed primarily for customers such as the Co-operative Dairies, Express Dairies, United Dairies and Wall's Ice Cream."* Whitby Morrison

Right: *The style of things to come, demonstrated by one of the new 'heart brand image' Transit mobiles.* David Hayward

Above: *The wild and remote wastes of the A6 as it passes over Shap in Cumbria, with an 18-pallet trailer T73. Even in the height of summer, Shap Fell can be a cold and chilly place, so there is little fear of the product getting spoiled, so perhaps Shap is the best place for a stop-over. Here we see a Scania LB110 (OFH 919L) on the long haul north. It is wearing the Wall's 'sunshine yellow' livery, but the paint looks like the standard Scania 'day-glo orange' of the early 1970s.* Chris Stevens Collection

Left: *The classic Wall's AEC Mammoth Major MkV, seen with its original body and illuminated front sign. Peter Tubwell recalls that this one, 3085 MT, was one of a batch of 30 such vehicles delivered in 1961. Note the driver's uniform.* L. Chick

Ice Cream In Bulk

Just as in the story of the manufacture of ice-cream products, the account of Wall's transport has its origins in the meat, sausage and pie side of the company's business. Back in 1876-7, just before his brother joined the management of the firm, Thomas Wall II was considering how to organise the rapidly expanding business. The biggest area for improvement did not however lay in the production or the quality of their goods, but in their delivery services. The company had two pony traps and a horse-drawn van back then, but a lot of deliveries were done with boys carrying large wicker baskets from door to door on a series of 'rounds'.

Above: *A 1926 Model TT Ford delivery van that was based at Acton in the 1920s; these vehicles (although insulated) were limited to a delivery route of under 50 miles, due to the fact this would take them about two hours to complete.* Wall's

This was not a very reliable way of doing business. Indeed, when passing through London, their delivery boys (some as young as 11) had been 'accosted and their wares stolen by blackguards.' Reading in a London newspaper of one such assault in 1876, a gentleman by the name of George Singer from Coventry presented himself at the Jermyn Street premises, 'to show to the Wall's brothers his new product, the delivery bicycloped.'

Singer had started his business in Warwickshire just the previous year, and he was keen to attract business in London, so he looked for all the openings and opportunities he could find. The footpad robberies of the mid-1870s had affected several leading businesses using delivery boys; so Singer told his potential customers, that 'their customers could now be supplied more resolutely than hitherto', and do so 'with a velocity that no footpad could intercede.'

A deal was struck, and over the years the meat business operated both delivery bikes and trikes, all of which were 'fitted with a tubular steel frame to hold wicker [sic] hampers.' By the early 1900s, the Singer company had also sold Wall's a number of motor-cycles, which were used to serve premises on the outskirts of the fast-growing city. Quite when the first motor-van was delivered is a matter of conjecture, but there is anecdotal evidence to suggest the first may well have been a motorcycle-van, again produced by Singer in Coventry.

During World War I, Wall's took delivery of some Ford Model T vans, which were then assembled at Trafford Park in Manchester, along with a larger Burford lorry. Vehicles were in short supply at this time, so the Burford had to be approved by the Minister of War Transport. It was kept busy 'working between the sausage works and the cannery at Isleworth.' After the war, when production finally settled down (and it must be remembered that many of the army units were not disbanded until 1920), business began to return to normal.

It was about this time that the company took an interest in ice-cream, and what could be more logical than to develop the sales of a luxury food treat, after so many years of hardship, death and privation. The meat company had, by this time a number of Model T Fords and five Burfords, which 'sat idle from noon on Saturday to 6am on a Monday morning. The venture into ice-cream production ensured that this would not last long, and soon the vans were working seven days a week.

Delivering ice-cream to stands and kiosks on Saturday afternoons and Sundays was satisfactory in the early stages, but the runaway success meant that the business soon needed more vans, and further Model T and TT Fords were acquired. These were fully insulated, and were used to stock a growing number of ice-cream depots as the 1920s progressed. Meat product vans were still used on a weekend, although these were mainly routed to ensure that the 'Walsie Trike' vendors had their stocks replenished. Model A, AA and BB Fords followed in the late-1920s and 1930s.

After World War II, and from about 1947, the delivery fleet grew rapidly, with the company initially standardising on Bedford chassis, in the K, M, O and OSS types. This was partly due to the fact that Bedford offered the company a much better financial deal, and partly because the Fordson 7V was considered a dated pre-war design. Chassis cabs were delivered direct to Wall's, and the bodying was split between Wadham Stringer, Hooper, Northern Counties and their own workshops.

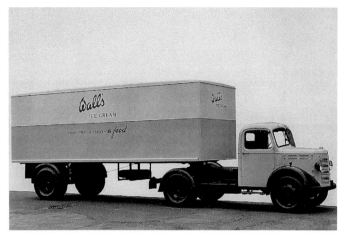

Left: *By the latter part of the 1920s, ice-cream delivery vans could manage journeys of up to 75 miles 'before their products began to go runny.' Faster speed and greater reliability was achieved with the Model AA Ford, of which a 1934 model is seen here. Interestingly, Sybill Dawson of Harlow recalls her father used to bring his home on a night, and there was always a few dishes of ice-cream to pass around the neighbours, as well as bottles of orange juice. Their next door neighbours were a butcher on one side, and a fishmonger on the other, and "that fair exchange was no robbery."* Wall's

Top and Middle Right: *The combination of the Bedford seven-ton short wheelbase tractor unit and the Scammell coupling system led to the OSS model. So, in 1947, an initial batch of ten of these were delivered with Scammell twin-rear-wheel trailer frames to Hooper & Son for bodying. Further batches would follow in 1948 and 1950.* Hooper Coachworks

Bottom Right: *After the war ended, there was a limitation on what use new vehicle chassis could be supplied for, as the motor manufacturers were faced with the Government order, 'Export or Die'. Ice-cream vans came low on the priority list, but ironically ice-cream delivery vans did not. Indeed, Wall's began to take an early priority in the vehicle acquisition stakes, as they were classed as a 'food manufacturer'. Here we see fleet number 1013, a Bedford MS two-ton chassis fitted with an insulated body.* Wall's

Top Left: *This Bedford a two-ton MS chassis/cab, was registered in Middlesex in 1948 and carries fleet number 1907. However the photograph appears to have been taken much later judging by the livery. Insulated box bodies, cooled by the addition of dry ice, were deemed to have a life of about seven years, whereas the chassis just four years, so the bodies were intended to be fitted to newer chassis until eventually disposed of.* Chris Stevens Collection

Middle Left: *Bedford TMY 631, fleet number 3037 dates to 1949 and appears to be K-Type 30-cwt chassis/cowl with an insulated coachbuilt delivery body possibly by Hawson. Note the lack of the large 'W' with the 'Wall's' script inside, possibly dating it to earlier than No.1907.* A. Cypher Collection

Bottom Left: *Bedford XMT 852, fleet number 5037 was new in 1952 and appears to have a Hooper-built insulated delivery body on an OLB five-ton chassis-cowl model.* Wall's

The factories at Acton and Godley near Manchester were 'bursting at their seams', so a new one opened at Craigmillar near Edinburgh in 1948 to handle the far north. This involved the running of 'night trunk lorries' up the A1 or A6, which was an arduous journey with a Bedford OSS in the immediate post-war years. According to Jack Sharpe: "Vehicle maintenance was the key to a 'sweet-running operation', and this was done in London. To reduce costs, the maintenance was shared with the Wall's meat vehicles fleet, at least until the two companies were formally separated in 1955."

Jack also recalls the arrivals of the Bedford's with great enthusiasm, saying: "I started as an apprentice mechanic at the age of 15 in 1935, and during the war years we had lorries of 1930 to 1938 vintage, their bodies were creaky, their mechanical parts worn out, and we had few spares with which to repair them. It literally was a question of sticking them together with string and sealing wax. Inside the van bodies, the floors were treacherous, as we were then carrying thousands of tons of margarine and cooking fat, plus another whale oil mixture, which was used to pack sausages in the tins we supplied to the armed forces. Once you had seen that, you never wanted to see (let alone eat) another sausage ever again. The Bedfords were a revelation, we got two in 1945 with squared tin fronts, just like the military lorries, and these did the work of three Fordsons. By 1948 we had a fleet of them, and every one came with a full set of spares included in the purchase price. It was just heaven to work on these trucks, and I'll never forget them."

The Bedford OSS tractor units were to prove extremely versatile, and over the latter part of the 1940s, they were the company's 'first-line' vehicles, not only working between Acton and the two satellite factories, but also between the factories and the depots as well. For instance, a lorry that drove from London to Manchester, would be away from its home base for two days, the driver being on what was called a 'lodging turn'. Peter Tubwell (Tubbie to his friends) stayed at the home of Jock Stringer in Mottram, Nr. Manchester, who worked in the Transport Department at Godley.

Whilst Peter rested up during the day, Jock was paid the lodging allowance in addition to his day rate as a 'storesman'. The two became good friends, and over a period of several months, Peter taught Jock to drive the OSS tractor, "quite unofficially of course." Jock then applied to become a driver, and surprised the Transport Manager by his driving skills. "Jock soon became a driver on the day runs, taking the OSS and a large 'Prestcold' freezer trailer out on bulk deliveries to Morecambe, Blackpool, Southport, Liverpool and then through the Mersey Tunnel to New Brighton, Wallasey and Chester." Peter remained a trunk driver until the early 1960s, but he lost touch with Jock after the Manchester factory closed, and would like to make contact (via the publishers of this book) with him or any of his old friends if they are reading it.

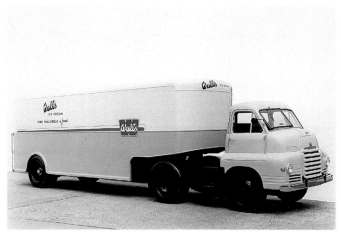

Top Right: *Wall's used Bedford SA Tractor units, and from 1954 their successor models the SAG (petrol-engined) and SAO (Perkins R6 diesel-engined) in both fleets. This is believed to be a model SA, with a chrome bumper and is coupled to a new Hooper-built refrigerated trailer. However some of the fleet had nearside spotlights fitted, which this unit does not have. Various trailer designs were used although at least one after the 1955 split in the divisions had an illuminated six-sided Wall's sign in the front. C. K. Bowers*

Centre Right: *This SA tractor unit, WMT 661, fleet number 8035, was registered in 1951 and was photographed on numerous occasions, as well as being the prototype for scale models. This unique tractor has a chromed grille and smaller bumper than similar units, and has streamlined bodywork with rear wheel covers. Vauxhall Motors*

Bottom Right: *Number 8035 was coupled to at least two multi-compartment refrigeration unit trailers and is seen here with doors opened. The tractor-trailer units were used at events to enable re-stocking of sales units. Vauxhall Motors*

Top Left: *The first of the new Bedford TD Type 30-cwt models, fleet number 1960 (711 HML) arrived in the Wall's fleet just before Easter 1956. It was one of a number of different vehicles registered in the 7xx HML series, including Austin tractor units, Morris LD vans and several cars.* Wall's

Middle Left: *This was another 1956 addition to the fleet but, as the number P100 suggests, it was a prototype. It never actually belonged to Wall's, but was loaned as a chassis cab model by Bedford, and fitted with a cold-store body for long-term evaluation.* Wall's

Bottom Left: *Another test-bed was this late-1958 acquisition, an early Bedford TJ fitted with a Perkins diesel engine. As 6270, it was used in Kent until January or February 1959, then re-registered and sent to work in Northern Ireland.* Wall's

Jack Sharpe also recalls the arrival of other Bedford models: "In 1950 I was allowed to visit the Commercial Motor Show at Earls Court, and was greatly impressed with the new Big Bedford, a five-ton model, with a very modern (bulbous) cab. The Chief Engineer liked them from the word go, and we placed orders for our 1951 deliveries with Luton, cutting back on some of the orders that were intended to go to Austin. The eight-ton S-Type Tractor Units with Scammell couplings looked so much better-equipped, and these proved ideal for the long runs up to Edinburgh and Manchester.

The new T-series was also of interest, and these came in two size options, a medium commercial up to three-ton with a 76bhp engine, and a four-tonner with an 84bhp engine. There were little models in the range, with payloads from one-ton to 30-cwt, and I suggested that these might be better for mobile sales units than the LDs we had on batch order from BMC. As it turned out, we stuck it out with the LD and found to our cost that these couldn't be successfully 'modernised' to take TVO generators for the Carpigiani machines.

The Chief Engineer also liked the idea of standardising on one manufacturer, as this would have made life much easier when it came to training mechanics and holding spares. The management disagreed, on the principle that it was better 'not to put all your eggs in one basket.' So we stayed with BMC for the 'mobiles' and started to use Bedford and Ford for the delivery fleet, although these were supplemented by Austin, Commer-Karrier, Morris and three Seddon 30-cwt vans, which were used at the Manchester Depot. These were very reliable little models, and they partly influenced the decision to buy Seddon later on.

In 1956-7 we switched to an up-rated TA, the TD, which was introduced following weight regulation changes in 1956. Yet, the TD was only an interim step towards the TJ that would be introduced to the fleet in 1959. In late-1956 Bedford offered us a test model for evaluation, and this was fleet P100. It had a Perkins diesel engine and several parts and modifications that would be fitted to the TJ when it was launched at the 1958 Commercial Motor Show. Nevertheless, it was a TD model, as is obvious from the picture opposite, despite the fact that it has since been described in one vintage vehicle magazine as a J4.

I drove this vehicle quite a lot in its first month with the fleet, including several runs to Scotland via Lancashire. I bet this was the only time a van with a cold storage body was ever used to deliver office stationery. The diesel engine was problematic however, as was 6270 that followed two years later, where we were plagued with minor, but annoying difficulties.

Nowadays fleet operators will swear by diesel engines, but half a century ago, we were still on a learning curve. If the truth is told, perhaps the problems lay with the fitters and the drivers rather than the engines themselves. But back then, we really loved those big Bedford petrol engines, with their American-designed blocks. When coupled to a Bedford gearbox, you could tell them coming back into the garage from a quarter of a mile away. I can still hear them now."

Below: *A normal-control (diesel) Bedford TJ, with a cold store body. These were used to deliver to Wall's retail customer outlets, and were known as 'merchandise units'. A salesman/ driver would use one of these vans on a prescribed route, re-stocking retailers freezer cabinets as they went. A safety release catch was fitted on the inside of the rear door to prevent the driver being locked in.* Wall's

Top Left: *This 1960 Bedford TJ is possibly fitted with a dry-ice cooled coachbuilt body, and has the registration 104 M. It is pictured here, on Madeira Drive in Brighton in 1961 at the Brighton Coach Rally, but quite what it is doing there is not known. Note that the van does not have a fleet number, as their application and usage seems to have tailed off.* ATPH/NA3

Middle Left: *This 1960 Bedford TJ chassis-cowl 935 UMV, fleet number 1571, has been fitted with another type of insulated coachbuilt body for distribution work. Yet, this is unlike that fitted to previous bodies, as it has a refrigeration unit with an opening access panel. However, as with the non-refrigerated bodies, dry ice was used although in this case it was to primarily help out the unit in summer.* Whitby Morrison

Bottom Left: *This 1960 Bedford J-type (5632 MK) appears to have the same body as 104 MV although has been in service for longer, and is pictured in perhaps 1963-4 on a delivery from a distribution depot to a West Country confectionery shop with a Wall's concession.* Chris Steven's Collection

Given their experience with the TA and then the TD chassis, it is no surprise that Wall's acquired a chassis-cab model on trial, and then followed this up with large orders for chassis-cowl versions for delivery from the 1960 season onwards. The significance of these orders was shown by a new Wall's-liveried TJ, with the company's own bodywork, being exhibited on the Bedford stand at the 1960 Commercial Motor Show.

It appears that the first TJ delivered was a chassis-cab test-bed, fitted with a Perkins diesel engine and insulated box body (dry ice cooled?) for delivery work. Despite the problems with diesel engines at this time, Wall's evidently decided to concentrate on an all-diesel fleet with the commensurate fuel savings. Apart from replacing the Bedford tractor units' petrol-engines with Perkins or Leyland diesel engines, all of the new TJ chassis were apparently Perkins engine-equipped.

Many of the chassis-cowl versions were bodied with Wall's own 140-can or 150-can bodywork as 'merchandising units', complete with sliding cab doors both sides for ease of entry/exit. The bodies were very similar to those fitted to Wall's new Ford Thames Trader chassis-cowls. All were intended for salesmen/drivers to use on routes from the distribution depots to retailers for restocking their freezers. However all the pictures of that body type show an Onan 5kva generator unit behind a small door on the offside rear powering refrigeration, although supplementing with dry ice was often required.

Above: *As Wall's purchased a large number of normal-control TJ chassis they also acquired the new forward-control chassis from Bedford, the TK series introduced for the 1960 Model Year. Fleet number 1000 is shown when new supplied as a chassis-cab and bodied with a non-refrigerated box body that seems to be very similar to that on the TJ number 6270.* Wall's

Right: *A rear view showing the single door. These bodies had an intended life of seven years, the chassis just four. When General Franco closed the border between Spain and Gibralta in 1969, several redundant box bodies were purchased from Wall's and used on the 'Rock' as temporary cold stores, Wall's also supplied the colony with several ex-Whippy van TVO generators to power them.* Wall's

Top Left: *Turning now to Ford chassis in the Wall's fleet, this is a Fordson Thames D4 chassis-cowl (251 JMX) of 1956, fleet number 2443. It is fitted with another type of coachbuilt insulated delivery body. Note the cut-out on the nearside door and single rear wheels.* Wall's

Bottom Left: *This D4 chassis-cowl with twin rear wheels has a similar 150-can insulated body to that fitted to Bedford and Morris chassis. However, please note the number, 82523; this has the '8' prefix that was applied to some vehicles (apparently after the 1955 separation with the meat business). This shows the company policy at the time to purchase various makes for delivery chassis, and also fit standard body types.* Wall's

Top Right: *This generator may well be an Onan 5kv and is installed in fleet number 1530 (seen below) and other similar 'refrigerated' vehicles, all of which used TVO generators. Note the hand-operated fire extinguisher in front and the hefty battery for the electric self-starter* Wall's

Bottom Right: *This Fordson Thames D4 twin rear wheel chassis-cowl was registered in the summer of 1958 with 92 SMH, becoming fleet number 1530. It is the first of the new coachbuilt bodies equipped with a refrigeration unit in the front nearside of the body. It has a hinged access panel with grille affording ventilation and a TVO tank below. It is believed that as the unit occupied a large part of the body the capacity was reduced to 130 cans. The driver would probably have been required to add dry ice in summer.* Wall's

Top Left: *The successor to the D4 was the Thames Trader, available initially in forward-control only. The chassis cab for 1599 was supplied in 1959 and bodied in January 1960 by Smiths (of Gateshead?) for the Bulk Supply Fleet. It will be seen that it has a long box-type insulated body taking advantage of the forward position of the cab.* Whitby Morrison

Middle Left: *This second Trader (with registration 987 VMX) was delivered new in the summer of 1959, but the chassis was completely rebuilt in the Gloucester workshops, whilst the original body was refurbished in April 1964. Note, however that there is no fleet number, and the new 'Wall's ICE CREAM' shield and no red 'W' on the waistband.* Whitby Morrison

Bottom Left: *A rear view of 987 VMX showing the application of the 'Wall's shield' on the single rear door.* Whitby Morrison

In 1959, Wall's did a study on the life-span of their van bodies, as it was becoming apparent that their working life was by then reduced. A change from ash-framed bodies to ones of composite materials saw the life-span being rapidly reduced. Quite literally they were "shaking themselves to bits", said Jack Sharpe. The advent of the new Bedford TJ model and the Ford Thames Trader offered a chance to address this, as these chassis were quite well-suited to another kind of treatment, namely the 'box van body'. These bodies could be produced as separate units, and if required could be de-mounted from one chassis and placed on another. This resolved a major problem, that of chassis life expectancy.

Whilst a chassis could happily do several years in service, Wall's reckoned that anything beyond 54 months was not cost-effective, as the costs of maintenance and replacement parts rose dramatically once a medium-weight commercial vehicle reached its fourth anniversary. This had been especially pronounced on the Bedford TA and TD models and also on the Fordson Ds. As some integral bodies were needing major work at the end of three years, and chassis required the same at the end of four years, it was clear that the disparity in maintenance schedules was becoming a serious difficulty. If the two could be separated, then this was clearly not a big issue, as bodies and chassis could be swapped at their respective overhaul dates. In this way, it was envisaged that a box van body may well even last up to eight years, and thus see out two chassis cabs if these were replaced on a four-year exchange programme.

Not all of the Ford Thames Traders carried the new box body styling as Jack Sharpe continues: "It had been decided that the box van body was still unproven as yet, and throughout the period 1960 to 1964, the idea was to body the fleet half and half. A lot of the Bedford TJs were going to Hawson direct from the factory at Luton, and these turned out to be slightly cheaper than we could produce in-house. As cost was a major consideration, it was decided that we should primarily concentrate on the Thames Trader chassis, as none of Ford's 'approved bodybuilders' could get their costs low enough.

However, we had a problem with the rear entry on our bodies, which at that time had a pair of slim two-leaf doors at the back. This gave a wide entry for a man carrying a tray of products, and was slightly wider than the single door eventually adopted. Yet, after a while in service, the rubber clips that held the door back against the body (when open) were prone to perish and weaken, and in a strong wind the doors would blow shut, causing all kinds of difficulties. We ultimately went to single-piece door therefore, and by the mid-1960s the separate box body and single door were more or less universal."

Around this time, the cost of coachbuilt products had accelerated considerably, and this was coupled to a dramatic decline in the numbers of coachbuilders around. Both of these were worrying trends for the companies that relied on such traditional bodies, as it was clear that by the 1970s, it would be extremely impractical to continue in this method. What is more, a traditional coachbuilt body was estimated as giving three to four years in service, whereas the life-span of a 'bolt-on' box body was estimated at around seven years, thanks to the fact that vibration from the chassis was reduced by rubber mountings.

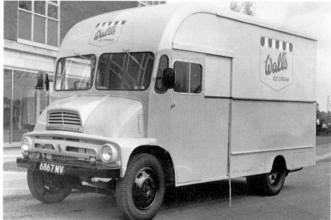

Top Right: *This 1960 Ford Thames Trader chassis-cowl has a coachbuilt insulated body for local deliveries from distribution depots, for which work it would be very similar to those fitted to other types of chassis. However, as it has the revised livery, and an 'in-service' appearance, the photograph was probably taken in the mid-1960s.* Chris Stevens Collection

Middle & Bottom Right: *Jack Sharpe recalls that this 1960 Trader entered the fleet for the 1961 season, and was originally fitted with a larger set of twin-leaf doors at the back. It was rebuilt and given the new livery, and is depicted at Gloucester in April 1964. However this may have been an experimental livery as the rear door has the 'Wall's rosette' (used on the meat and pie vehicles) with the six-sided badge and 'FIRST in FLAVOUR'.* Whitby Morrison

Top Left: *Wall's acquired further Ford chassis cab models for local deliveries, and they stuck with them through progressive model changes for several years. Depicted here is a new Ford D-series chassis-cab with GRP body in what was their then-current livery. All of this batch were purchased through Ford dealers Taylors of Gloucester in 1967-8 and carried Gloucester registrations. Note the large rear body overhang beyond the rear axle.* Whitby Morrison

Bottom Left: *This view shows the inside of the body with roof lights and compartments, plus the internal steps (for the driver to gain easy access), which had in turn been allowed for by that enormous overhang. It will also be seen that the door has a glass 'window', so that the nearside rear lights are visible from behind when the vehicle was parked and the door opened.* Whitby Morrison

Michael Moore, who was a Ford-trained mechanic, went to work for Wall's shortly after the D Series joined the fleet. He recalls: "The tip-over [tilt] cab was very comfortable to drive in, and they had a great deal of sound-proofing that was not found in comparable vehicles. Yet, there was a knack to getting these cabs to tip forward, and the gear lever had to be twisted in a certain way so that it did not foul the cab when this was being lowered back on to the chassis.. However, this must not have been fully explained to workshop personnel, as I was hired to work exclusively on these vehicles. Fifteen were laid up waiting for me in the workshop when I started there, and all of them had the same fault, a gear lever that had been bent flat by the cab being forced down when the lever was not in the right position."

Other faults existed with the fuel systems, and "the engine could be a swine to start as they needed priming. Cold mornings were also a devil, and to induce them to start we needed liberal quantities of 'Easi-Start'. The drivers just loathed these Fords, but it was more on the part of ignorance and an absence of a little TLC, rather than a real difficulty with the vehicles themselves. However, as can be seen in the pictures, the vans had long overhangs at their back end, and when fully loaded these gave the unpleasant sensation of the tail wagging the dog. Added to this, and in contrast to the TJ models, the chassis height was considerable and a series of steps had to be climbed to get into the main body of the vehicle, so the bad reputation continued. I eventually left Wall's for Greenham's of Isleworth, and then went to the Post Office who made much use of the D Series than Wall's, despite having far rougher drivers."

The purchase of Austin vehicles in the immediate post-war period was dictated not by the company's desire to get the right kind of vehicle for the job, but merely to get any kind of vehicle for the job. We have already touched on the position facing most vehicle manufacturers in the late-1940s, but we cannot stress strongly enough how much the Government's exhortation 'Export or Die' impacted on fleet operators in this country.

Due to the dire need to earn foreign currency in order to address the horrendous balance of payments and war-debt problems that Great Britain faced in 1946, it was essential that manufacturers did what they could to capture export orders. At this time the world needed trucks, and with the German, French and Italian automotive industries being decimated in the war years, British truck makers not only supplied the 'Empire' but most of Europe as well.

Above: *Wall's acquisition policy included BMC chassis for delivery work. This is believed to be an Austin Loadstar K4, circa 1954 and not the successor Austin version of the Morris WE. The chassis-cowl was bodied by Hooper but differs from that fitted to Bedford 5037, as it has been given a nearside loading door.* Wall's

Wall's were therefore forced to go to those manufacturers who could, a) initially supply conversions of military type vehicles and b) could offer production-line supplies within two years. The two companies that fitted this category were Austin of Longbridge and Bedford of Luton. Both of whom were, in turn, allowed to release 'forward allocations' to Wall's, as they were considered a foodstuff manufacturer, partially due to the fact that margarine production continued in London and Godley.

Top Left: *This is another photograph of the unique Hooper-bodied mobile sales and information unit forward-control Austin CXD Series II bus chassis, which was fitted with either an Austin petrol or a Perkins P6 diesel engine. On either side of a wide central gangway, it had insulated compartments to carry bulk supplies of products, including ice creams, sausages and pies. The back half was an open space, into which folding chairs and a table could be placed for use when the vehicle was at events. When it was travelling to a show, the space was used to carry 'Wallsie Trikes' that in turn would be stocked by the unit when it was at events.* C.K. Bowers

Middle Left: *Another photograph of a Hooper-bodied Austin K4 from the offside, the cab pressing on this vehicle was made by Airflow Streamline of Northampton, and as a consequence it has several characteristics that could be found in the Commer medium commercials of that day.* C.K. Bowers

Bottom Left: *When Austin and Morris merged in 1952, they formed the British Motor Corporation, and a fair amount of badge engineering went on as similar products were marketed as either Austin or Morris models. This is the Morris WE from Morris Commercial Cars, Birmingham, which used the Loadstar cab with Morris grille. BMC also offered an Austin three- to five-ton version with a different grille and badge. This chassis-cowl has the same style of body as was then being used on other types of chassis, and was registered in 1957. It has been allocated fleet number 84259, which was another example of an '8'-prefixed fleet number. Capacity would have been 140 aluminium cans, kept cool with dry ice.* Wall's

Before the British Motor Corporation was formed (as a result of the merger in 1952 of Austin Motors, Morris Motors and Morris Commercial Cars), the companies had been quite serious rivals. In turn, this had resulted in 'cost-cutting' on bulk orders in order to sell large quantities to fleet buyers. Wall's had naturally taken advantage of this and acquired both Austin and Morris-Commercial chassis for use as mobile sales units and for delivery work. Further orders followed post-merger for both Austin and Morris-Commercial heavy chassis, although after 1955 the latter had been re-badged as just 'Morris'; other chassis were available as either Austin or Morris versions with the same engines, though adorned with different grilles and badges. Wall's contracted with a few chosen coachbuilders to build specialist bodies, including Hooper (Coachbuilders) Ltd of Western Avenue, Acton, near the Wall's factory.

Prior to the 1955 split in their two main divisions (ice-cream and sausages and pies) Wall's used a unique vehicle (see page 24) bodied by Hoopers for use as a mobile sales and information unit. It was built on Austin's equivalent of the Bedford SB bus chassis, the CXB albeit with forward control, and was thus a model CXD with a 15-feet wheelbase. As it appears to be a post-1950 model, it was a Series II with either Austin 4-litre petrol or Perkins P6 diesel. Its roomy body had seats for personnel, insulated compartments, space for Walsie trikes and steps to afford access for customers.

The company also purchased a number of Austin Loadstar K4 normal-control chassis. These were bodied by Hoopers for delivery work, although it is not known if the company had any predecessor K9 chassis in addition to the K8 Three-Way vans.

The Loadstar cab was also used by Morris-Commercial to create a normal-control cab version of the Morris FE (Series III) and Austin-badged equivalent, which were purchased by Wall's so it was logical to acquire the normal-control updated chassis for deliveries. The Morris WE and Austin equivalent were introduced in 1955 and examples of at least the Morris version were acquired in the spring of 1957 ready for the season with very similar bodies to those with the side door that were fitted to Ford Thames and Bedford chassis. Overall,however, it can be generally said that the drivers did not like the BMC offerings and much preferred the Bedford vehicles in the fleet.

Top Right: *The tractor unit seen here is a new Morris (Commercial Cars) FE, or Series III of around 1955. It was a successor to the Series I and II, which were also available in the Austin guise. Note the front-hinged doors and new Morris grille and badge. The trailer has a Hooper-built insulated body.* C. K. Bowers

Middle Right: *This photograph was taken in the Hooper (Coachbuilders) Ltd works on the Western Avenue, Acton, West London, near the Wall's factory. In the centre is a new Morris FE and Hooper-built trailer alongside a Bedford chassis-cowl, which can be dated to 1955.* Vauxhall Motors

Bottom Right: *This Morris FE, registration 718 HML of spring 1956 also has a Hooper-built trailer, believed to be T1342. This unit took part, along with fellow FE (665 KMG - fleet number 81390) at the Slough round of the 1957 Lorry Driver of the Year competition. This vehicle, 718 HML was originally fleet number 1342 and then renumbered to 81342 as seen in this photograph.* Wall's

We now turn to the AEC vehicles in the Wall's fleet, because as business expanded it became necessary to increase haulage capacity. The answer was to procure eight-wheeler chassis with twin front axles and forward-control cabs, in order to maximise capacity. At that time, AEC in Southall had a proven product range with reliable diesel engines with a large warranty and repair facilities and parts department, all of which was just a short distance away from Acton.

The aluminium ice cream containers of the day were known colloquially as 'cans' and a typical local delivery vehicle of the 1950s or '60s had a capacity of up to 150 cans. However, the articulated trailers had a much larger capacity and were known as '12', '13' or '14' trailers, such as the Hooper-built insulated

dry-ice trailers used behind the Bedford or Morris tractors. These articulated trailers had a capacity of 1,200, 1,300 or 1,400 cans; hence the designation. Yet, the variety of '13' trailers was less than the other types. Ice lollies and bricks were sold in cartons, two of which equalled one can. Local delivery vehicles might have up to a half-can and half-carton load, but larger deliveries were generally either cans or cartons. The need for higher capacity resulted in an order for a single Mammoth Major Mark III (683 WHC), which (after approval) was followed by several batches of Mark Vs, all of them equipped with Park Royal Vehicles' coachbuilt cabs. Ultimately an AEC subsidiary, this firm were better known for its bus bodies, even though they had long produced commercial vehicle cabs and bodies.

Left: *Wall's acquired AEC Mammoth Major V (3791) in 1960, with a Park Royal cab for bulk deliveries. The small badge at the back indicates the insulated, non-refrigerated body was built by Smiths, and it carries a paint date of 30th January 1960. Note the original body style, which like earlier 'merchandising' vans has twin-leaf rear doors.* Wall's

Top Right: *Another 1960-delivered Mammoth Major V registration 9194 MK (possibly fleet number 3785) shows that the original aluminium can box bodies had an illuminated six-sided Wall's sign, as did some earlier articulated trailers.* Chris Stevens Collection

Middle Right: *Next we have a 1961 Mammoth Major V, photographed at a transport café on the A3, although it was obviously taken post-1964, as the chassis has had a new body fitted. Note that it also has the new 'shield' livery, and not the illuminated one; this makes this a GRP '12-pallet box body' from Mickleover. Note the lack of a fleet number.* H. Gates

Bottom Right: *This photograph is of a 1966 AEC Mandator tractor unit registration GFH 117D. It has an 18-pallet metal body trailer, number T70, possibly pictured in late-1968, at Membury Services. These trailers supplemented the earlier type.* A. Cypher

The known fleet list suggests the Mammoth Major chassis originally had insulated 'Box Van' bodies with a 2,000-can capacity. Photographs of the original bodies show that they were broadly similar in their ribbed-side styling to those fitted to contemporary Thames Trader chassis-cabs. They had sufficient differences to suggest it was a different bodybuilder (albeit one working to Wall's plans), and this may have been Smiths of Gateshead.

The bodies also had an illuminated six-sided 'Wall's ICE CREAM' sign very similar to those on some earlier trailers. The illuminated signs were apparently the idea of a Wall's director who had seen proposals presumably by London Transport's Advertising Department to use illuminated signs on the new London buses. Wall's were already advertising on bus sides and this proposal seems to coincide with the development of the Routemaster. An illuminated sign was added to several trailers and then (in due course) on the mobile sales vehicles. After the initial Mammoth Major MkIII, the MkV chassis were delivered and registered in at least seven, with known registration dates from 1960 to 1961.

According to Peter Tubwell, one batch of 36 MkVs included two for the biscuit company (registered 3842,5 MT) in 1961, which he believes were operated by sister company SPD and fitted with pantechnicon bodies; the total payload of these trucks full of biscuits and cones was about three-tons. However, the biscuit delivery arrangements, although interesting, really form part of another, much larger story..

Based on the good record of the larger AECs, Wall's acquired a small batch of AEC Mercury box vans for their Gloucester-West Country runs, but they proved too expensive to purchase and operate, so they were disposed of after just one season. After 1964 some of the eight-wheel AECs were fitted with new Mickelover 12-pallet GRP bodies, although some were still in the original form until at least 1968, because Acton (for instance) was not able to cope with pallets. In due course some survivors were sold to Edwards of Lydbrook (e.g. 134 MV) and then converted to 4x2 tractor units for sale. Pat 'Terry' Spinks recalls returning with another driver in April 1964 who promptly ran into a bus in Coventry, although this AEC was repaired.

In early-1966, AEC supplied a batch of Mandators, which were coupled to new Mickelover-bodied 12-pallet box trailers, augmented by metal 18-pallet trailers by 1968. About half the AECs had their original 11.3-litre AV691 engines replaced with 12.47-litre AV760 units, the first being GFH 108D.

As with the Mammoth Majors, the Mandators had front wing 'rubbing strips'! Mandator mirror arms were originally positioned on the cab doors, but this was found to impair vision and attract road spray, so they were repositioned on the windscreen pillar! Although some Mandators were written off through accidents, survivors were repainted in the yellow 'sunny days' livery, e.g. GFH 111-2D and GFH 108D, which was a depot Shunter, were all active in July 1975. However pioneer GFH 101D was not, and it was eventually cannibalised in 1974.

Below: *This 1966 Ergomatic-cabbed AEC Mandator tractor unit (GFH 101D) is outside the AEC, Southall Works, in West London. The articulated body is the original design, produced in GRP suitable for up to 12 pallets.* AEC

Acton started to convert to palletisation by 1968, although the process may have continued to the early-1970s. To replace the rigid eight-wheelers, Wall's ordered new tractor units for 1970 delivery. All received Gloucester registrations; the first Scania LB110 tractors, plus Seddon 32-4 units supplied by Prails of Hereford. Some of the Seddons at least were coupled to ex-BRS flatbed trailers, which then received the Mickelover GRP box bodies that had been removed from the AEC Mammoth Major V chassis. The 12- and 18-pallet trailers continued in service.

Some Seddons were also rented from BRS, although they lacked power-assisted steering that was found on the Wall's-owned versions. Wall's had had a small number of Seddons in the 1950s and this experience coupled with the concerns over the Ford D-type tractors, specifically their gearboxes, led to

Above: *After several years in service, the Mickleover-built GRP bodies were removed from the defunct AEC MkV chassis and worked by the new Seddons.* Chris Stevens Collection

their selection of a reliable chassis, engine (Gardner or Rolls Royce), gearbox (David Brown) and comfortable cab. Alan Earnshaw, then with David Brown, remembers dealing with this order from Seddons, as it was stated that Wall's "were seeking complete reliability in both power units and transmission." The 1970 models had their instruments and dials positioned in the centre of the dash panel and windscreen wipers under the windscreen, whereas the 1971 models had the former in front of the steering wheel and latter above the windscreen! Both the 32-4s and LB110 units had 'Bostrom' driver's suspension seats.

Above: *This Scania LB110 tractor registration OFH 916L, dating to December 1973, is coupled to a metal 14-pallet trailer T51. Two batches of the Scania tractors were delivered in the blue livery and the next in the new 'sunny days' yellow livery. Most vehicles were re-liveried accordingly, though a few (e.g. AEC GFH 101D, cannibalised in 1974) were never re-painted.* CPM

Left: *The fact that the chassis cab and box van body became widely used, is shown in this picture of a 1978 Dodge Commando with registration UFH 841S. It is fitted with the Hi-Line cab and was used for local deliveries, much as the merchandising and retail vans of the 1950s and '60s. The front of the box van clearly advertises Cornettos, but while the side panels carry the 'sunshine logo', they are difficult to see.* Chris Stevens Collection

The 1970s were a troubled time for the British motor manufacturing industry, especially at British Leyland who owned AEC. Indeed, during 1979 British Leyland's decided to stop manufacturing AECs. Wall's had of course tried Leyland products; for instance, back in 1968 they had acquired a batch of Beavers with semi-automatic gearboxes. They also had some 1975-6 Terrier 850 Box Vans and they later had Leyland Roadtrain tractor units. But the success with the Scania LB110s led them to order further batches from Unit Commercials of Salisbury (though wearing Gloucester registrations) and they primarily hauled the new 14-pallet metal trailers.

These were succeeded by more batches of LB111 units, N-registration to V-registration, followed by X-registered P112 units delivered on 9th June 1982. Illustrated on page 50, is a 1978 Dodge Commando 9.7-ton Box Van, of which several were purchased. Wall's also invested in Mickleover-built insulated bodies for the new British Rail Freightliner container trains, which could also be used on road trailers. In 1983/4 the company had delivered DAF 3300 and then Leyland Cruiser 6 x 2 twin-steer Box Vans (C and D-registrations). However in 1986 the Unilever merged their Wall's and Bird's Eye frozen foods divisions and this resulted in wholesale vehicle fleet changes, which again are far too numerous to detail in this book.

Top Right: *This photograph shows the cab of a Bedford TK tractor unit coupled to a 'Venetian Bridge' publicity trailer advertising the Cornettos in the late 1970s. The combination is believed to be at Plymouth.* Stuart Whitby

Bottom Right: *Mickleover made GRP-bodies for Wall's, including that seen on page 50. For a time Birds-Eye Wall's tried insulated bodies operated by British Rail's Freightliner division, which were able to be loaded onto road trailers or Freightliner wagons for distribution. This was not altogether a success story, and was shortly abandoned.* Stuart Birkby

ACKNOWLEDGEMENTS

This book has only been due to the kind assistance and fond memories of a number of people in the ice-cream industry, and the authors are deeply indebted to: -

Alfred Baker
Stuart Birkby
Ronald & Doreen Davies
Sybill Dawson
Neil Fraser
H. Gates
Roland Gill
Russell Harvey
Donald Hayle
Rick Jones
Leo Kane
Robert Neil
Michael Moore
Tom Pickersgill
Steve Pheasant
Daisy & Ken Reynolds
Jack Sharpe
B. Smith
Douglas Smith
Steve and Lynette Smith
Pat 'Terry' Spinks
Rob Stuart
Steve Tillyer
Peter Tubwell
P.B. Walters
Bryan & Stuart Whitby

Above: *Here we see a 1978 Scania LB111 (registration UFH 866S) tractor unit eastbound from Gloucester on the A40. It is coupled to a 16-pallet spread axle trailer number T86, which was used for bulk deliveries from the Gloucester works.*
J. Proctor

Information Appeal

Much of the information in this book has been gathered from Wall's employees past and present, but there is a greater story yet to tell and far more information to uncover; this is only the 'tip of the ice-lolly' so to speak. If you have any additional memories or photographs of Wall's or Mr.Whippy-liveried vehicles, the authors would be delighted to hear from you. Please write to the editorial (Appleby) address shown on page two of this book, or e-mail us at: -

admin@transpenninepublishing.co.uk